Prayer
Catholic Couples

With Reflections
from Pope Francis'
The Joy of Love

REBEKAH AND COLEMAN

Compiled and Edited by Susan Heuver

MAY THIS BOOK BE AN
INSTRUMENT TO DRAW YOU
CLOSER TO EACH OTHER AND
TO GOD AND A REMINDER
THAT YOU ARE LOVED BY
GRANDMA + GRANDPA HAYES

the**WORD**
among us®
press

7-29-17

Published by The Word Among Us Press
7115 Guilford Drive, Suite 100
Frederick, Maryland 21704
www.wau.org

21 20 19 18 17   1 2 3 4 5

ISBN: 978-1-59325-306-6
eISBN: 978-1-59325-491-9

Cover design by David Crosson
Photo courtesy of Anthony Amsberry

Made and printed in the United States of America

Library of Congress Control Number: 2016952988

Contents

Thinkstock Photos

Introduction

It is my hope that, in reading this text, all
will feel called to love and cherish family life,
for "families are not a problem; they are first and
foremost an opportunity."

—POPE FRANCIS, *AMORIS LAETITIA*, 7

On April 8, 2016, Pope Francis released his long-awaited apostolic exhortation on the family, *Amoris Laetitia* (The Joy of Love). Archbishop Joseph E. Kurtz, president of the U.S. Conference of Catholic Bishops, welcomed the exhortation as a "love letter to families . . . inviting all of us . . . to never stop growing in love." *Amoris Laetitia* is an exhortation in the purest sense; Pope Francis passionately urges families to renew their zeal and devotion to building marriages that both experience and reflect the love of Christ, which brings joy to families and joy to the Church.

As my husband and I read this letter, we immediately sensed the Holy Father's compassion toward all families. Pope Francis writes from his heart and seems to base his comments on real conversations with real married couples, perhaps at the dinner table or in the confessional. These are not pious platitudes. On the contrary, his pastoral concern for married couples is palpable. In this beautiful letter, the Holy Father provides practical wisdom and encourages couples to recognize the beauty of married life and God's comforting presence in their own imperfect families.

We especially found chapter 4, which focuses on 1 Corinthians 13, to be both inspiring and challenging, calling us to a more sacrificial love in our own marriage and parenting. As we have tried to see each other through the eyes of God, to lovingly accept each other as we are, and to repent and forgive each other often, we have grown closer to Christ and to one another. To our delight, even after twenty-seven happy years of marriage, we are experiencing even greater joy in our life together.

At 264 pages, *The Joy of Love* is a lengthy work. In writing *Prayers for Catholic Couples,* I hope to provide an accessible means for couples to read and meditate on Pope Francis' message together and grow in their love for one another. He himself did not recommend a "rushed reading of the text" but intended, rather, that families read prayerfully and carefully, paying particular attention to those parts relevant to their specific needs (*Amoris Laetitia*, 7). This book is designed to be used by couples in exactly this way, one reflection at a time. Each two-page spread includes a brief quote from *Amoris Laetitia*, a reflection question, and a short prayer for the couple to say together. Couples should not feel as if they have to use the book in the order the chapters are presented. They can choose whichever reflection most speaks to their life at that moment.

All married couples experience stress at times. Although we know that we ought to seek God's help especially during those times, many couples find it difficult to pray together. It can feel awkward to know where to begin or what to say. So experiment with how to pray together. You don't necessarily have to pray the entire reflection together. For example, you might want to use each reflection in this book in your personal prayer time first, journaling answers to the questions provided, and then come together later in the day to talk about your insights and pray the prayer together. Or you can come together after your personal reflection, join hands, and just pray spontaneously about your hopes and dreams for your marriage and family.

I hope that by using *Prayers for Catholic Couples*, married couples can begin or deepen their experience of family prayer. By spending even ten minutes with your spouse to seek God's blessing for your family, lives can change, love can grow, and relationships can be transformed by God's grace. I pray that you and your spouse will be encouraged and full of hope that God is present and working in your family, even in the midst of the very real stresses of family life.

Susan Heuver

The Life of Our Family

God Is Present in Our Messiness

A Gift and a Sign

This Exhortation . . . represents an invitation to Christian families to value the gifts of marriage and the family, and to persevere in a love strengthened by the virtues of generosity, commitment, fidelity, and patience. . . . [I]t seeks to encourage everyone to be a sign of mercy and closeness wherever family life remains imperfect or lacks peace and joy.

—*AMORIS LAETITIA, 5*

Reflect

How much do you value the gift of marriage and family? How can you persevere in love? How can you be a sign of mercy to others?

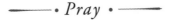

Pray

Father of every family, I invite you into the messy imperfection of our family. Open our eyes to see signs of your closeness. Dispel any discouragement and increase our hope for the future. Use us, Lord, to bring your closeness to other families who are facing difficulties. Fill us with peace and joy as we persevere in our love for one another.

"Families Are an Opportunity"

It is my hope that, in reading this text, all will feel called to love and cherish family life, for "families are not a problem; they are first and foremost an opportunity" (Address at the Meeting with Families in Santiago de Cuba, September 22, 2015).

—*AMORIS LAETITIA*, 7

Reflect

What about your family life do you cherish? Where do you need God's grace to see your family as an opportunity and not as a problem?

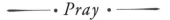

Pray

Father, thank you for the joy that we experience through our family. Thank you for the blessings of love and laughter, of companionship and support. In those areas that we find difficult, send your grace. Help us to see our family's life together as a blessing and an opportunity, not as a problem or a trial.

Jesus' Comforting Presence

Jesus himself was born into a modest family that soon had to flee to a foreign land. He visits the home of Peter, whose mother-in-law is ill (cf. *Mk* 1:30-31) and shows sympathy upon hearing of deaths in the homes of Jairus and Lazarus (cf. *Mk* 5:22-24, 35-43; *Jn* 11:1-44). He hears the desperate wailing of the widow of Nain for her dead son (cf. *Lk* 7:11-15) and heeds the plea of the father of an epileptic child in a small country town (cf. *Mk* 9:17-27). . . . Jesus knows the anxieties and tensions experienced by families and he weaves them into his parables: children who leave home to seek adventure (cf. *Lk* 15:11-32), or who prove troublesome (*Mt* 21:28-31) or fall prey to violence (*Mk* 12:1-9). He is also sensitive to the embarrassment caused by the lack of wine at a wedding feast (*Jn* 2:1-10), the failure of guests to come to a banquet (*Mt* 22:1-10), and the anxiety of a poor family over the loss of a coin (*Lk* 15:8-10).

— *Amoris Laetitia*, 21

—— • *Reflect* • ——

Jesus accompanied and comforted many suffering families in Scripture. How has Jesus comforted your family? Where do you need his comforting presence today?

—— • *Pray* • ——

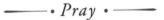

Jesus, you visited and healed the sick, grieved over the dead, comforted mourners, and visited outcasts. You know well the tensions we experience daily in our family. Come with your presence and your comfort. Help us to be aware of your presence in the midst of our suffering. Remind us that you are always with us through your word in Scripture, your Body and Blood in the Eucharist, and through your people in the body of Christ, the Church.

Look to the Holy Family

Every family should look to the icon of the Holy Family of Nazareth. Its daily life had its share of burdens and even nightmares, as when they met with Herod's implacable violence. This last was an experience that, sad to say, continues to afflict the many refugee families who in our day feel rejected and helpless. Like the Magi, our families are invited to contemplate the Child and his Mother, to bow down and worship him (cf. *Mt* 2:11). Like Mary, they are asked to face their family's challenges with courage and serenity, in good times and bad, and to keep in their heart the great things which God has done (cf. *Lk* 2:19, 51). The treasury of Mary's heart also contains the experiences of every family, which she cherishes. For this reason, she can help us understand the meaning of these experiences and to hear the message God wishes to communicate through the life of our families.

AMORIS LAETITIA, 30

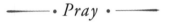

· *Reflect* ·

What challenge in your family life are you facing right now in which you need more courage and serenity? How can the Holy Family's example help you?

· *Pray* ·

Father, be with our family as we navigate our challenges. Teach us to trust in your plans and remember your faithfulness. We put our sufferings and fears, our hopes and dreams, into your hands. Be with everyone who suffers, especially those who are alone. Make our family, like the Holy Family, a place of prayer and love—and a refuge for others who suffer. Mary, help us to ponder, as you did, the meaning of our experiences, especially when we don't fully understand the circumstances in our lives.

God Dwells in Families

The Lord's presence dwells in real and concrete families, with all their daily troubles and struggles, joys and hopes. Living in a family makes it hard for us to feign or lie; we cannot hide behind a mask. If that authenticity is inspired by love, then the Lord reigns there, with his joy and his peace. The spirituality of family love is made up of thousands of small but real gestures. In that variety of gifts and encounters which deepen communion, God has his dwelling place.

—*AMORIS LAETITIA*, 315

—— • *Reflect* • ——

What "gestures"—perhaps a kind look, thoughtful word, or a kiss or hug—deepen communion in your family? What other small actions (perhaps praying the Rosary, grace at meals) could help your family experience more of God's presence in your home?

—— • *Pray* • ——

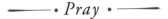

Lord, thank you for dwelling in our very own family, with all its daily troubles and joys. Thank you that we can come to you transparently, with our messiness, without hiding behind a mask of false perfection. Please guide us as we seek to make our home your dwelling place. Inspire us with signs of thoughtfulness and kindness so that our family continues to grow in our love for you and one another.

There Is No Perfect Family

[N]o family drops down from heaven perfectly formed; families need constantly to grow and mature in the ability to love. This is a never-ending vocation born of the full communion of the Trinity, the profound unity between Christ and his Church, the loving community which is the Holy Family of Nazareth, and the pure fraternity existing among the saints of heaven. Our contemplation of the fulfillment which we have yet to attain also allows us to see in proper perspective the historical journey which we make as families, and in this way to stop demanding of our interpersonal relationships a perfection, a purity of intentions, and a consistency which we will only encounter in the Kingdom to come. It also keeps us from judging harshly those who live in situations of frailty. All of us are called to keep striving toward something greater than ourselves and our families, and every family must feel this constant impulse. Let us make this journey as families; let us keep walking together. What we have been promised is greater than we can imagine. May we never lose heart because of our limitations, or ever stop seeking that fullness of love and communion which God holds out before us.

—*AMORIS LAETITIA*, 325

· *Reflect* ·

How does recognizing that your family is called to constantly grow and mature bring you peace and help you to stop demanding perfection of yourself, your spouse, and your children?

· *Pray* ·

Lord, help us to remember that no family is perfect, and that you dwell with us in our imperfection. Give us hope and courage to keep walking together. We need your grace today and every day. Come, walk beside us, and transform us into the couple and the family you have created us to be.

Paying Attention to Our Loved Ones

We can be fully present to others only by giving fully of ourselves and forgetting all else. Our loved ones merit our complete attention. Jesus is our model in this, for whenever people approached to speak with him, he would meet their gaze, directly and lovingly (cf. *Mk* 10:21). No one felt overlooked in his presence, since his words and gestures conveyed the question: "What do you want me to do for you?" (*Mk* 10:51). This is what we experience in the daily life of the family.

—*AMORIS LAETITIA,* 323

——— • *Reflect* • ———

Have I ever felt overlooked by my spouse? Am I at times too busy to pay attention to my spouse and children? How can I give them my complete attention?

——— • *Pray* • ———

Lord Jesus, you never wearied of giving others your full attention. Help us not to be too tired or preoccupied to pay attention to each other. Our human love is finite, but your love is infinite and enduring. Pour your unchanging love into our hearts so that we look lovingly at each other and express concern in word and action.

Mothers: Witnesses to Tenderness

"Mothers are the strongest antidote to the spread of self-centered individualism. . . . It is they who testify to the beauty of life." Certainly, "a society without mothers would be dehumanized, for mothers are always, even in the worst of times, witnesses to tenderness, dedication, and moral strength. . . . Without mothers, not only would there be no new faithful, but the faith itself would lose a good part of its simple and profound warmth. . . . Dear mothers: thank you! Thank you for what you are in your family and for what you give to the Church and the world" (Catechesis, January 7, 2015).

—*AMORIS LAETITIA*, 174

——— · *Reflect* · ———

What did your mother or grandmother teach you about love? How can you be (or help your wife to be) a witness to tenderness?

——— · *Pray* · ———

Mary, Mother of the Church, you were the mother and first teacher of the Son of God. Pray for me (or my wife), that I (or she) would bring the tenderness and generous love of God to our family. Father in heaven, thank you for the gift of mothers. Pour out a special grace of strength and selfless love today upon my wife (or upon me) so that our home may be a place where family and friends experience your faithful, tender love, especially in times of difficulty.

To Be a Father Is to Be Always Present

God sets the father in the family so that by the gifts of his masculinity he can be "close to his wife and share everything, joy and sorrow, hope and hardship. And to be close to his children as they grow—when they play and when they work, when they are carefree and when they are distressed, when they are talkative and when they are silent, when they are daring and when they are afraid, when they stray and when they get back on the right path. To be a father who is always present" (Catechesis, February 4, 2015).

—*AMORIS LAETITIA*, 177

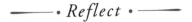

Reflect

How has your father or your husband brought blessing to your family? How can you, as a man, reflect God's fatherhood to your family? How can you, as a woman, support your husband in his role as a father to your family?

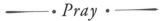

Pray

Lord, you are Father to the fatherless. Raise up strong men of faith who will show your love to their families. Thank you for the fathers in our lives—biological, adoptive, or spiritual. Bless these men. Affirm them in their call and capacity to reflect your fatherhood to their children and to the world.

Mothers and Fathers Reveal the Face of God

Every child has a right to receive love from a mother and a father; both are necessary for a child's integral and harmonious development. As the Australian Bishops have observed, each of the spouses "contributes in a distinct way to the upbringing of a child. Respecting a child's dignity means affirming his or her need and natural right to have a mother and a father" (Australian Catholic Bishops' Conference, Pastoral Letter, *Don't Mess with Marriage*, November 24, 2015). We are speaking not simply of the love of father and mother as individuals, but also of their mutual love, perceived as the source of one's life and the solid foundation of the family. Without this, a child could become a mere plaything. Husband and wife, father and mother, both "cooperate with the love of God the Creator, and are, in a certain sense, his interpreters" (Vatican II, *Gaudium et Spes*, 50). They show their children the maternal and paternal face of the Lord. Together they teach the value of reciprocity, of respect for differences, and of being able to give and take. If for some inevitable reason one parent should be lacking, it is important to compensate for this loss, for the sake of the child's healthy growth to maturity.

—*AMORIS LAETITIA*, 172

———— · *Reflect* · ————

How do mothers and fathers contribute to the upbringing of their children in ways that are distinct and unique, yet complement one another? Why are both important?

———— · *Pray* · ————

Lord, we want to each reveal your face to our children. Help us always respect each other's differences and support one another as we parent our children. Keep our eyes open to opportunities to support single parents as they seek to provide the formation that their children need.

The Treasure of Grandparents

Very often it is grandparents who ensure that the most important values are passed down to their grandchildren, and "many people can testify that they owe their initiation into the Christian life to their grandparents" (*Final Report of the Synod of Bishops*, 2015, 18). Their words, their affection, or simply their presence help children to realize that history did not begin with them, that they are now part of an age-old pilgrimage, and that they need to respect all that came before them.

—*Amoris Laetitia*, 192

——— · *Reflect* · ———

How has a grandparent or elderly person enriched
and influenced your life? How can your family reach
out to and embrace the elderly?

——— · *Pray* · ———

Lord, thank you for our parents and grandparents.
We are grateful for all they have taught us. Bless abun-
dantly all the elderly for the many sacrifices they have
made. Help us to show them reverence and respect,
not only for what they have done in the past, but
also for the beautiful witness they continue to provide. Give us opportunities to listen to older men and
women, to hear and appreciate their wisdom, and to
show them that they are loved.

Remembering the Past

Listening to the elderly tell their stories is good for children and young people; it makes them feel connected to the living history of their families, their neighborhoods, and their country. A family that fails to respect and cherish its grandparents, who are its living memory, is already in decline, whereas a family that remembers has a future.

—*AMORIS LAETITIA*, 193

—— · *Reflect* · ——

What is a memorable story that you recall from your grandparents? When was the last time you or your children had this kind of conversation with a grandparent or elderly person?

—— · *Pray* · ——

Lord, the elderly have such wisdom to share. Sometimes it is hard for us to find the time to sit and have meaningful dialogue with our parents or grandparents. Provide us with opportunities to listen to their stories. Holy Spirit, give us the questions to ask that will prompt our elderly relatives to share about their lives. We want to cherish our grandparents and the memories they have to share, knowing that this "living history" will give us perspective for the future.

Cherishing In-Laws

One particularly delicate aspect of love is learning not to view [in-laws] as somehow competitors, threats, or intruders. The conjugal union demands respect for their traditions and customs, an effort to understand their language and to refrain from criticism, caring for them and cherishing them while maintaining the legitimate privacy and independence of the couple. Being willing to do so is also an exquisite expression of generous love for one's spouse.

—*AMORIS LAETITIA*, 198

———— • *Reflect* • ————

How do we each care for and respect our in-laws?
How might we grow in deeper understanding of them
and their ways?

———— • *Pray* • ————

Lord Jesus, you cured Peter's mother-in-law and
showed care and respect for all those you encoun-
tered. Help us to grow in love and understanding
for each other's parents and siblings. Though we did
not grow up in these families, we have been joined
with them in marriage. May we see our in-laws now
as our own loved ones. Help us to remember that in
loving our in-laws, we are also loving our spouse.

Special Needs Children: Gifts to the Family

"Families who lovingly accept the difficult trial of a child with special needs are greatly to be admired. They render the Church and society an invaluable witness of faithfulness to the gift of life. In these situations, the family can discover, together with the Christian community, new approaches, new ways of acting, a different way of understanding and identifying with others, by welcoming and caring for the mystery of the frailty of human life. People with disabilities are a gift for the family and an opportunity to grow in love, mutual aid, and unity" (*Final Report of the Synod of Bishops*, 2015, 21).

—*AMORIS LAETITIA*, 47

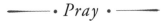

· Reflect ·

Think about a family with one child or more with specials needs—it may be your own. How has the presence of that child enriched and blessed that family?

· Pray ·

Father, you love every person you created. Thank you for the unique gifts and qualities that you've given to our family members. Thank you for families who have welcomed a child with special needs and for the generous witness they give to the world. Bless them, and give them strength and joy as they care for one another. Help us to encourage and support these families.

Caring for Those Who Are Grieving

At times family life is challenged by the death of a loved one. We cannot fail to offer the light of faith as a support to families going through this experience. To turn our backs on a grieving family would show a lack of mercy. . . . I can understand the anguish felt by those who have lost a much-loved person, a spouse with whom they have shared so much. Jesus himself was deeply moved and began to weep at the death of a friend (cf. *Jn* 11:33, 35). And how can we even begin to understand the grief of parents who have lost a child? "It is as if time stops altogether: a chasm opens to engulf both past and future," and "at times we even go so far as to lay the blame on God. How many people—I can understand them—get angry with God" (Catechesis, June 17, 2015).

—*Amoris Laetitia*, 253, 254

———— • *Reflect* • ————

How have you experienced the support of the Church after the death of a loved one? What can you do to extend the love of Christ to those who mourn?

———— • *Pray* • ————

Lord, death is a great struggle for us who remain behind. We miss our loved ones deeply and at times don't understand why they had to die. Help us as spouses to support each other in times of grief and to point one another toward you, our loving Father. May our family be a refuge for those who mourn. May we welcome into our home those who've lost a family member and support them as they rebuild their lives.

The Heavenly Banquet

If we accept death, we can prepare ourselves for it. The way is to grow in our love for those who walk at our side, until that day when "death will be no more, mourning and crying and pain will be no more" (*Rev* 21:4). We will thus prepare ourselves to meet once more our loved ones who have died. Just as Jesus "gave back to his mother" (cf. *Lk* 7:15) her son who had died, so it will be with us. Let us not waste energy by dwelling on the distant past. The better we live on this earth, the greater the happiness we will be able to share with our loved ones in heaven. The more we are able to mature and develop in this world, the more gifts will we be able to bring to the heavenly banquet.

—*AMORIS LAETITIA*, 258

Reflect

Have you and your spouse talked about death? What would help you to have more peace as you think about your death or the death of your spouse?

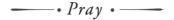

Pray

Lord, you give us each other for a period of time on this earth. Help us to treasure one another lovingly and to live without regret. Give us confidence that one day we will see our loved ones again. In this sure and certain hope, may we live in trust and generosity, with eyes fixed on heaven and hands ready to serve those around us.

Growing in Our Love

Grace for Each Step of the Way

The Grace of the Sacrament

[T]he love between husband and wife, a love sanctified, enriched, and illuminated by the grace of the sacrament of marriage . . . combines the warmth of friendship and erotic passion, and endures long after emotions and passion subside. Pope Pius XI taught that this love permeates the duties of married life and enjoys pride of place (Encyclical Letter *Casti Connubii*, 23). Infused by the Holy Spirit, this powerful love is a reflection of the unbroken covenant between Christ and humanity that culminated in his self-sacrifice on the cross. "The Spirit which the Lord pours forth gives a new heart and renders man and woman capable of loving one another as Christ loved us. Conjugal love reaches that fullness to which it is interiorly ordained: conjugal charity" (John Paul II, Apostolic Exhortation *Familiaris Consortio*, 13).

—*AMORIS LAETITIA*, 120

——— • *Reflect* • ———

How have you seen the Holy Spirit make you or your spouse capable of a level of sacrificial love that is greater than your own human capacity? Where do you need grace for self-sacrifice today?

——— • *Pray* • ———

Lord Jesus, you laid down your very life for us. This type of love and sacrifice is challenging. Sometimes, Lord, we don't want to sacrifice for our spouse because we are tired or annoyed or think it's "their turn" to be the one to sacrifice. Send your Spirit into our hearts so that we can love one another in the way that you have loved us: without limit, pouring out all that we are for the other.

Lifelong Marriage: a Gift, Not a Yoke

"The indissolubility of marriage—'what God has joined together, let no man put asunder' (*Mt* 19:6)— should not be viewed as a 'yoke' imposed on humanity, but as a 'gift' granted to those who are joined in marriage. . . . God's indulgent love always accompanies our human journey; through grace, it heals and transforms hardened hearts, leading them back to the beginning through the way of the cross" (*Report of the Synod of Bishops*, 2014, 14).

—AMORIS LAETITIA, 62

——— • *Reflect* • ———

What helps you to view the permanent and lifelong aspect of your marriage as a "gift" from God rather than as a "yoke" or a burden? How do you experience God's love healing your wounds and softening your heart?

——— • *Pray* • ———

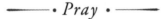

Lord Jesus, your closest disciples betrayed and denied you, abandoning you in your hour of need. You understand how difficult it can be to love "even unto death." By your grace, help us to see our marriage as a gift, to be merciful to one another, and to hold onto the divine love that you have given us to sustain our unity. Restore to us the joy of our first love for each other as we recommit ourselves to one another each day.

Cultivating the Joy of Love

In marriage, the joy of love needs to be cultivated. . . .
Marital joy can be experienced even amid sorrow; it
involves accepting that marriage is an inevitable mixture of enjoyment and struggles, tensions and repose,
pain and relief, satisfactions and longings, annoyances
and pleasures, but always on the path of friendship,
which inspires married couples to care for one another.

—*AMORIS LAETITIA*, 126

——— • *Reflect* • ———

What brings you joy? What brings your spouse joy? How can the two of you "cultivate" joy together?

——— • *Pray* • ———

Lord Jesus, you know well the challenges of family life—you were poor, your friends misunderstood and betrayed you, and you suffered a humiliating death. Yet you had an infectious joy that attracted many to follow you. Help us to cultivate an atmosphere of joy in our home by treasuring one another, laughing together, and spending time together doing the things that bring each other happiness, even amid life's realities.

In Good Times and Bad

Gradually, "with the grace of the Holy Spirit, [the spouses] grow in holiness through married life, also by sharing in the mystery of Christ's cross, which transforms difficulties and sufferings into an offering of love" (*Final Report of the Synod of Bishops*, 2015, 87). Moreover, moments of joy, relaxation, celebration, and even sexuality can be experienced as a sharing in the full life of the resurrection.

—*AMORIS LAETITIA*, 317

Reflect

In what ways do you experience the "mystery of Christ's cross" and the "full life of the resurrection" in your marriage? In your family?

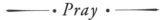

Pray

Holy Spirit, by your grace, help us to become more like Jesus through our daily challenges. Transform every mundane task into an offering of love by your presence in our hearts. Help us to recognize and seize the moments of joy that you offer us each day. Thank you for the gift of living together as a family.

A Gaze of Love

[L]ove is expressed in that "gaze" which contemplates other persons as ends in themselves, even if they are infirm, elderly, or physically unattractive. A look of appreciation has enormous importance, and to begrudge it is usually hurtful. How many things do spouses and children sometimes do in order to be noticed! Much hurt and many problems result when we stop looking at one another. This lies behind the complaints and grievances we often hear in families: "My husband does not look at me; he acts as if I were invisible." "Please look at me when I am talking to you!" "My wife no longer looks at me, she only has eyes for our children." "In my own home nobody cares about me; they do not even see me; it is as if I did not exist." Love opens our eyes and enables us to see, beyond all else, the great worth of a human being.

—*Amoris Laetitia*, 128

——— • *Reflect* • ———

How often do you experienced a "gaze" of love from someone in your family? How often do you give that look of love?

——— • *Pray* • ———

Loving Father, thank you for the gift of one another and for the gift of our family. Open our eyes to see each member of our family as you do. Show us their great worth in your eyes. Soften our hearts toward them so that we view them with eyes of mercy. Help us to look at them lovingly, to speak to them tenderly, and to reach out to them with gestures of love and kindness. Give us a fresh outpouring of grace so that we might appreciate and serve one another in joy and love.

Love Grows through Pain and Sorrow

[J]oy also grows through pain and sorrow. . . . After suffering and struggling together, spouses are able to experience that it was worth it, because they achieved some good, learned something as a couple, or came to appreciate what they have. Few human joys are as deep and thrilling as those experienced by two people who love one another and have achieved something as the result of a great, shared effort.

—*AMORIS LAETITIA, 130*

—— • *Reflect* • ——

What is one obstacle that you and your spouse have overcome together? Can you see that it "was worth it" now? How can this perspective help you today?

—— • *Pray* • ——

Heavenly Father, sometimes life is so busy that we forget to look back and recognize what you have done. Thank you for helping us to face and overcome challenges together. Teach us to pause and recall your faithfulness as well as the faithfulness we have shown one another. Let this bring us joy and remind us to gladly persevere together as we face today's sufferings and challenges.

The Patience of a Craftsman

Fostering growth means helping a person to shape his or her own identity. Love is thus a kind of craftsmanship. . . . In the life of married couples, even at difficult moments, one person can always surprise the other, and new doors can open for their relationship, as if they were meeting for the first time. At every new stage, they can keep "forming" one another. Love makes each wait for the other with the patience of a craftsman, a patience which comes from God.

—*AMORIS LAETITIA*, 221

—— · *Reflect* · ——

In what positive ways have we formed one another? How patient are we with the process?

—— · *Pray* · ——

Father, thank you for giving us to each other so that we can grow in you. Give us a docile and teachable spirit so that we are open to change. Help us to realize that our marriage will continue to grow as we do. Give us patience, especially in the difficult moments. May we cooperate with you, the Master Craftsman, and your plan for our lives.

God Uses Our Spouses to
Help Us Mature

[M]arried life is a process of growth, in which each spouse is God's means of helping the other to mature. Change, improvement, the flowering of the good qualities present in each person—all these are possible. Each marriage is a kind of "salvation history," which from fragile beginnings—thanks to God's gift and a creative and generous response on our part—grows over time into something precious and enduring. Might we say that the greatest mission of two people in love is to help one another become, respectively, more a man and more a woman?

—*Amoris Laetitia*, 221

Reflect

How has your spouse made you more of a man or more of a woman of God? How can you help your spouse grow in holiness and become the man or woman God has created him or her to be?

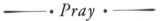

Pray

Lord, we thank you for one another. You have given us to each other to walk together in our journey toward you. Help us to value the differences that we each possess and to recognize the ways in which these differences are a blessing to our family. Keep both of us from trying to "change" the other; rather, help us to delight in each other. Through our love, help us bring each other closer to you and to the man and woman of God you desire us to be.

Love Needs Time and Space

Love needs time and space; everything else is secondary. Time is needed to talk things over, to embrace leisurely, to share plans, to listen to one other and gaze in each other's eyes, to appreciate one another and to build a stronger relationship. Sometimes the frenetic pace of our society and the pressures of the workplace create problems. At other times, the problem is the lack of quality time together, sharing the same room without one even noticing the other. . . . [M]arried people should think of ways to . . . make the most of those moments, to be present to one another, even by sharing moments of meaningful silence.

—*AMORIS LAETITIA, 224*

—— • *Reflect* • ——

Do we enjoy spending time together? What gets in the way of "couple time"? How can we make the most of the time that we do have together?

—— • *Pray* • ——

Lord, we want our love to grow. Help us to carve out time to spend together for fun, for prayer, for talking and listening, and for doing "nothing" at all. We want to enjoy the gift of time that you have given us to refresh us and to deepen our love. Help us not to turn to other things but instead turn to you and each other for joy and companionship.

Know How to Spend Time Together

Once a couple no longer knows how to spend time together, one or both of them will end up taking refuge in gadgets, finding other commitments, seeking the embrace of another, or simply looking for ways to flee what has become an uncomfortable closeness.

—*AMORIS LAETITIA*, 225

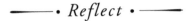

Reflect

Do you observe yourself or your spouse ever wanting to "flee" from being at home or being together? If so, what makes each of you feel this way? What do you turn to at times like that?

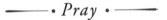

Pray

Lord, give us courage to identify and speak openly about those times when we find being together unpleasant or too hard. Change our hearts when we want to run to pleasure or isolation or distraction instead of to each other. Only you can fill our deepest needs—these things will not satisfy us anyway. Fill us with your grace so that we desire time with both you and our spouse.

Building Bonds of Love

Young married couples should be encouraged to develop a routine that gives a healthy sense of closeness and stability through shared daily rituals. These could include a morning kiss, an evening blessing, waiting at the door to welcome each other home, taking trips together, and sharing household chores. Yet it also helps to break the routine with a party, and to enjoy family celebrations of anniversaries and special events. We need these moments of cherishing God's gifts and renewing our zest for life. As long as we can celebrate, we are able to rekindle our love, to free it from monotony, and to color our daily routine with hope.

—*AMORIS LAETITIA, 226*

—— • *Reflect* • ——

What builds a sense of closeness and stability for you? What builds it for your spouse? What can you add to your daily routines to bring greater closeness and build unity in your marriage?

—— • *Pray* • ——

Jesus, you traveled with your disciples, shared meals with them, told stories, celebrated at weddings, grieved together, and prayed together with them. Help us to do these things together and build bonds of love. Give us creative ways to cherish one another and rekindle our love. Increase our hope and expectation for our future together.

Overcoming Crises Can Strengthen Marriage

The life of every family is marked by all kinds of crises, yet these are also part of its dramatic beauty. Couples should be helped to realize that surmounting a crisis need not weaken their relationship; instead, it can improve, settle, and mature the wine of their union.

—*AMORIS LAETITIA*, 232

———— • *Reflect* • ————

What is the biggest challenge you are facing right now? What support do you need, together and individually, to overcome this challenge? What can you do to ensure that it strengthens, not weakens, your marriage?

———— • *Pray* • ————

Lord Jesus, you know the hardships we are facing. You have the answers we need and the power to resolve them. Bring us through these challenges so that we are even closer to one another than we were before. We put these situations into your hands. Protect our unity, and give us your wisdom as we work through issues and make decisions. Help us to speak kindly to each other and listen well. May we resolve conflict respectfully and always make decisions with special concern for our children.

Seeking and Granting Forgiveness

[T]here are those personal crises that affect the life of couples, often involving finances, problems in the workplace, emotional, social, and spiritual difficulties. Unexpected situations present themselves, disrupting family life and requiring a process of forgiveness and reconciliation. In resolving sincerely to forgive the other, each has to ask quietly and humbly if he or she has not somehow created the conditions that led to the other's mistakes. Some families break up when spouses engage in mutual recrimination, but "experience shows that with proper assistance and acts of reconciliation, through grace, a great percentage of troubled marriages find a solution in a satisfying manner. To know how to forgive and to feel forgiven is a basic experience in family life" (*Report of the Synod of Bishops*, 2014, 44).

—*Amoris Laetitia*, 236

—— • *Reflect* • ——

How much are asking for and granting forgiveness a regular part of your marriage? If you struggle to forgive your spouse, do you turn to prayer and the sacraments for help?

—— • *Pray* • ——

Jesus, you came to earth and suffered on the cross so that our sins might be forgiven. Give us the grace we need to forgive one another, and grant us the humility to ask for forgiveness when we have hurt each other, even if we think it was just a minor offense. Let the beauty of mercy and forgiveness permeate our marriage relationship.

Faithfulness: A Matter of the Heart

Marriage is also the experience of belonging completely to another person. Spouses accept the challenge and aspiration of supporting one another, growing old together, and in this way reflecting God's own faithfulness. . . . At the same time, such fidelity would be spiritually meaningless were it simply a matter of following a law with obedient resignation. Rather, it is a matter of the heart, into which God alone sees (cf. *Mt* 5:28). Every morning, on rising, we reaffirm before God our decision to be faithful, come what may in the course of the day. And all of us, before going to sleep, hope to wake up and continue this adventure, trusting in the Lord's help. In this way, each spouse is for the other a sign and instrument of the closeness of the Lord, who never abandons us: "Lo, I am with you always, to the close of the age" (*Mt* 28:20).

—*AMORIS LAETITIA*, 319

——— • *Reflect* • ———
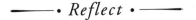

How is your spouse's enduring and faithful love an instrument and sign to you of the goodness and closeness of the Lord? How can you be such a sign?

——— • *Pray* • ———

Lord, thank you for giving us each other, a faithful spouse who freely and gladly chooses to belong completely to me and walk beside me in my journey of life. Today we declare once again that we choose each other, come what may. Help us to love generously and, through our love, be a sign of your closeness to our family. Thank you for your presence in our lives, now and always.

Difficulties Can Be Opportunities to Renew Love

It is becoming more and more common to think that, when one or both partners no longer feel fulfilled, or things have not turned out the way they wanted, sufficient reason exists to end the marriage. Were this the case, no marriage would last. At times, all it takes to decide that everything is over is a single instance of dissatisfaction, the absence of the other when he or she was most needed, wounded pride, or a vague fear. Inevitably, situations will arise involving human weakness and these can prove emotionally overwhelming. One spouse may not feel fully appreciated, or may be attracted to another person. Jealousy and tensions may emerge, or new interests that consume the other's time and attention. Physical changes naturally occur in everyone. These, and so many other things, rather than threatening love, are so many occasions for reviving and renewing it.

—*Amoris Laetitia*, 237

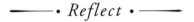

Reflect

Do you ever experience feelings of disappointment or a lack of fulfillment with your marriage? Why? How can you express these feelings constructively with your spouse or a trusted counselor?

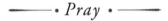

Pray

Lord, help us not to fear or give up when very real challenges or wounds or disappointment causes us to struggle to love. You know what we are experiencing, and you can transform these situations. Make them opportunities to reconnect as a couple so that we can recommit to loving one another. Give us wisdom and mercy, and wise counselors, as we seek to understand and care for each other. Restore and increase the joy in our marriage. Your grace in our marriage will see us through these issues and renew our love.

Reaffirming the Choice of Our Spouse

[S]ome have the maturity needed to reaffirm their choice of the other as their partner on life's journey, despite the limitations of the relationship. They realistically accept that the other cannot fulfill all their cherished dreams. Persons like this avoid thinking of themselves as martyrs; they make the most of whatever possibilities family life gives them and they work patiently at strengthening the marriage bond. They realize, after all, that every crisis can be a new "yes," enabling love to be renewed, deepened, and inwardly strengthened. When crises come, they are unafraid to get to the root of it, to renegotiate basic terms, to achieve a new equilibrium, and to move forward together. With this kind of constant openness they are able to face any number of difficult situations.

—*AMORIS LAETITIA*, 238

—— • *Reflect* • ——

How often do you reaffirm your choice of one another? How are you able to move forward together, despite difficulties and crises?

—— • *Pray* • ——

Heavenly Father, every day is a gift from you. Give us courage and hope as we encounter crises together and face our own limitations. We freely and whole-heartedly reaffirm our choice of our spouse. Help us to speak words of covenant love and to demonstrate our commitment and our love for one another as we move forward together.

The "Fine Wine" of Love

A word should also be said about those whose love, like a fine wine, has come into its own. Just as a good wine begins to "breathe" with time, so too the daily experience of fidelity gives married life richness and "body." Fidelity has to do with patience and expectation. Its joys and sacrifices bear fruit as the years go by and the couple rejoices to see their children's children. The love present from the beginning becomes more conscious, settled, and mature as the couple discovers each other anew day after day, year after year. Saint John of the Cross tells us that "old lovers are tried and true." They "are outwardly no longer afire with powerful emotions and impulses, but now taste the sweetness of the wine of love, well-aged and stored deep within their hearts" (*Spiritual Canticle* B, XXV, 11). Such couples have successfully overcome crises and hardships without fleeing from challenges or concealing problems.

—*Amoris Laetitia*, 231

——— • *Reflect* • ———

How have you experienced joy and a deepening of love through the years? How can you and your spouse "discover each other anew" day by day?

——— • *Pray* • ———

Lord, thank you for the witness given by long-married couples who have overcome hardships and continue to deepen in their love. Help us to look for the fruit of our own sacrificial love in our marriage and our parenting. Show us how to continually find delight in one another as we grow old together.

Only God Can Satisfy All Our Needs

There comes a point where a couple's love attains the height of its freedom and becomes the basis of a healthy autonomy. This happens when each spouse realizes that the other is not his or her own, but has a much more important master, the one Lord. No one but God can presume to take over the deepest and most personal core of the loved one; he [God] alone can be the ultimate center of their life. At the same time, the principle of spiritual realism requires that one spouse not presume that the other can completely satisfy his or her needs . . . [and] to stop expecting from that person something which is proper to the love of God alone. This demands an interior divestment. The space which each of the spouses makes exclusively for their personal relationship with God not only helps heal the hurts of life in common, but also enables the spouses to find in the love of God the deepest source of meaning in their own lives. Each day we have to invoke the help of the Holy Spirit to make this interior freedom possible.

—*AMORIS LAETITIA*, 320

———— • *Reflect* • ————

How can your prayer life strengthen your relationship with Christ and prevent you from having unreasonable expectations for your spouse?

———— • *Pray* • ————

Loving Father, thank you for the gift of my spouse, who brings great joy into my life. Show my husband/wife your love today. Help both of us to seek time alone with you in prayer to strengthen our relationship with you. You are my rock; you alone meet my deepest needs. Free me from thinking that my spouse can satisfy my deepest needs, which only you alone can do.

The Fruit of Our Love

God's Precious Gift of Children

A Living Reflection of the Triune God

The couple that loves and begets life is a true, living icon . . . capable of revealing God the Creator and Savior. For this reason, fruitful love becomes a symbol of God's inner life. . . . Seen this way, the couple's fruitful relationship becomes an image for understanding and describing the mystery of God himself, for in the Christian vision of the Trinity, God is contemplated as Father, Son, and Spirit of love. The triune God is a communion of love, and the family is its living reflection.

—*AMORIS LAETITIA*, 11

· Reflect ·

How does your family reflect the self-giving and fruitful love of the Trinity? How can you share your love beyond your immediate family?

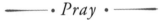

· Pray ·

Father, Son, and Holy Spirit, you are a Trinity of love. You constantly pour your love into your sons and daughters. Open our family to receiving your love. Fill us so that our love can be fruitful and bring life to others. Come, Holy Spirit, and fill us with your love so that we, too, can be a communion of love: loving one another and those around us and so revealing your goodness.

Each Child Is Unique and Irreplaceable

"Children are a gift. Each one is unique and irreplaceable. . . . We love our children because they are children, not because they are beautiful, or look or think as we do, or embody our dreams. We love them because they are children. A child is a child" (Catechesis, February 11, 2015). The love of parents is the means by which God our Father shows his own love.

—*AMORIS LAETITIA*, 170

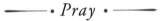

Reflect

In what ways does your love for your children mirror the love of God for them? How do you love them unconditionally? If you don't have children, how did your own parents show you the love of God?

Pray

Father, we thank you for the family that you have given us. Each one of them is your gift. Teach us to treasure them. Help us to love them unconditionally, just as you love us. Help us to notice their strengths and the joy they bring into the world. May we be the means through which our children come to know your love.

God's Dream Come True

Each child has a place in God's heart from all eternity; once he or she is conceived, the Creator's eternal dream comes true. Let us pause to think of the great value of that embryo from the moment of conception. We need to see it with the eyes of God, who always looks beyond mere appearances.

—*AMORIS LAETITIA*, 168

———— • *Reflect* • ————

How can I grow in seeing others with the "eyes of God," especially unborn children, people with disabilities, the elderly, the sick, and the dying?

———— • *Pray* • ————

Father of all, every person you create is a dream for you come true. Sometimes we don't see or value others in the way that you do. Open our eyes to recognize the value of everyone you have created in your image, especially unborn children. With every person we encounter, show us what you see so that we can love them as you love us.

The Great Value of a Human Life

Here I feel it urgent to state that, if the family is the sanctuary of life, the place where life is conceived and cared for, it is a horrendous contradiction when it becomes a place where life is rejected and destroyed. So great is the value of a human life, and so inalienable the right to life of an innocent child growing in the mother's womb, that no alleged right to one's own body can justify a decision to terminate that life.

—*AMORIS LAETITIA*, 83

Reflect

What might you, as a family, do to help protect the lives of unborn babies? How can your family be more open to life in your home?

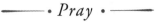

Pray

Father, you love every human being you have created. Give me your heart for the unborn, the elderly, the vulnerable, the homeless, and those who have no voice. Show our family how to be a welcoming sanctuary for all your children.

Through Children,
God Renews the World

The clear teaching of the Second Vatican Council still holds: "[The couple] will make decisions by common counsel and effort. Let them thoughtfully take into account both their own welfare and that of their children, those already born and those which the future may bring. For this accounting they need to reckon with both the material and the spiritual conditions of the times as well as of their state in life. Finally, they should consult the interests of the family group, of temporal society, and of the Church herself. The parents themselves and no one else should ultimately make this judgment in the sight of God" (Vatican II, *Gaudium et Spes*, 50). Moreover, "the use of methods based on the 'laws of nature and the incidence of fertility' (*Humanae Vitae*, 11) are to be promoted, since 'these methods respect the bodies of the spouses, encourage tenderness between them, and favor the education of an authentic freedom' (*Catechism of the Catholic Church*, 2370). Greater emphasis needs to be placed on the fact that children are a wonderful gift from God and a joy for parents and the Church. Through them, the Lord renews the world" (*Final Report of the Synod of Bishops*, 2015, 63).

—*AMORIS LAETITIA*, 222

——— • *Reflect* • ———

What can work against seeing children as a gift and not a burden? How do you avoid such a mentality, even as you carefully pray about the size of your family?

——— • *Pray* • ———

Father, thank you for the gift of our children and of all the young people in our family and the Church. Help us, and all parents, to be open to new life and to see children as a gift and not a burden. Give us the grace to pass on our faith. Form our children into men and women who will serve generously to renew the Church and the world in whatever state in life to which God calls them.

Adoption Is an Act of Love

Adoption is a very generous way to become parents. I encourage those who cannot have children to expand their marital love to embrace those who lack a proper family situation. They will never regret having been generous. Adopting a child is an act of love, offering the gift of a family to someone who has none.

—*AMORIS LAETITIA*, 179

———— • *Reflect* • ————

How has my family witnessed the generous love of God through families with adopted children? What might God desire to do in our family through foster care or adoption?

———— • *Pray* • ————

Lord, bless all families who have welcomed foster or adopted children. Thank you for the witness of their love. Help our family to grow in generosity so that we can be a place of welcome for neighbors, friends, and those in need. Give us discernment as we seek to know your will for our family.

Reaching Beyond Our Own Family

We also do well to remember that procreation and adoption are not the only ways of experiencing the fruitfulness of love. Even large families are called to make their mark on society, finding other expressions of fruitfulness that in some way prolong the love that sustains them. Christian families should never forget that "faith does not remove us from the world, but draws us more deeply into it. . . . Each of us, in fact, has a special role in preparing for the coming of God's kingdom in our world" (Address at the Meeting with Families in Manila, January 16, 2015). Families should not see themselves as a refuge from society, but instead go forth from their homes in a spirit of solidarity with others. In this way, they become a hub for integrating persons into society and a point of contact between the public and private spheres. Married couples should have a clear awareness of their social obligations. With this, their affection does not diminish but is flooded with new light.

—*AMORIS LAETITIA*, 181

—— • *Reflect* • ——

How can my family reach out to care for and positively influence those around us?

—— • *Pray* • ——

Jesus, you embraced our humanity and walked among us as a man. Help us to reach out beyond our own family to share your love. Show us the small, practical steps we can take to welcome others into our lives. We want to be spiritually fruitful in our neighborhood, parish, workplace, and community. May our love spill over into the world as we prepare for the coming of your kingdom.

The Gift of Family Hospitality

Led by the Spirit, the family circle is not only open to life by generating it within itself, but also by going forth and spreading life by caring for others and seeking their happiness. This openness finds particular expression in hospitality, which the word of God eloquently encourages: "Do not neglect to show hospitality to strangers, for thereby some have entertained angels unawares" (*Heb* 13:2). When a family is welcoming and reaches out to others, especially the poor and the neglected, it is "a symbol, witness, and participant in the Church's motherhood" (John Paul II, Apostolic Exhortation *Familiaris Consortio*, 141).

—*AMORIS LAETITIA*, 324

——— • *Reflect* • ———

How has a family with a gift of hospitality blessed
you or others? How can your family develop this gift
of reaching out to others?

——— • *Pray* • ———

Lord, help our family to have your generous love
for the poor, neglected, or lonely. Show us how to
open our hearts and our home to others so that we
can show them your love and bring joy to their lives.
Remind us that we do not need to be a perfect family
or have the perfect home to be welcoming to others.
May we be models for our children that our family
is one that cares for others.

A Place for the Poor

[O]pen and caring families find a place for the poor and build friendships with those less fortunate than themselves. In their efforts to live according to the Gospel, they are mindful of Jesus' words: "As you did it to one of the least of these my brethren, you did it to me" (*Mt* 25:40). In a very real way, their lives express what is asked of us all: "When you give a dinner or a banquet, do not invite your friends or your brothers or your kinsmen or rich neighbors, lest they also invite you in return, and you be repaid. But when you give a feast, invite the poor, the maimed, the lame, the blind, and you will be blessed" (*Lk* 14:12-14). You will be blessed! Here is the secret to a happy family.

—*AMORIS LAETITIA* 183

———— • *Reflect* • ————

How can we find a place for the poor in the life of our family? How can we build an authentic relationship with someone in need?

———— • *Pray* • ————

Lord, thank you for the blessings of our family and our home. Open our hearts to those who are less fortunate than we are. Give us your wisdom so that we may open our home to the poor and those in need. Show us how to build true friendships with these brothers and sisters whom you love.

Caring for the Wider Family

The nuclear family needs to interact with the wider family made up of parents, aunts and uncles, cousins, and even neighbors. This greater family may have members who require assistance, or at least companionship and affection, or consolation amid suffering. The individualism so prevalent today can lead to creating small nests of security, where others are perceived as bothersome or a threat. Such isolation, however, cannot offer greater peace or happiness; rather, it straightens the heart of a family and makes its life all the more narrow.

—*AMORIS LAETITIA* 187

——— • *Reflect* • ———

How often are we tempted to isolate ourselves as a family and perceive others as bothersome or a threat? How might God want our relationships with extended family members to grow?

——— • *Pray* • ———

Lord, show us how you are asking us to grow in loving our extended family members. Keep us from being so absorbed by our own family that we grow isolated from their needs. Help us always to remain in unity with one another as we discern together how to best care for our parents and siblings.

Hear the Cry of the Elderly

"Do not cast me off in the time of old age; forsake me not when my strength is spent" (*Ps* 71:9). This is the plea of the elderly, who fear being forgotten and rejected. Just as God asks us to be his means of hearing the cry of the poor, so too he wants us to hear the cry of the elderly. This represents a challenge to families and communities, since "the Church cannot and does not want to conform to a mentality of impatience, and much less of indifference and contempt, towards old age. We must reawaken the collective sense of gratitude, of appreciation, of hospitality, which makes the elderly feel like a living part of the community. Our elderly are men and women, fathers and mothers, who came before us on our own road, in our own house, in our daily battle for a worthy life" (Catechesis, March 4, 2015). Indeed, "how I would like a Church that challenges the throwaway culture by the overflowing joy of a new embrace between young and old!" (Catechesis, March 11, 2015).

—*AMORIS LAETITIA*, 191

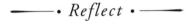

· Reflect ·

Can you think of an elderly person who might be lonely? How is God asking you to hear the cry of the elderly?

· Pray ·

Heavenly Father, so much of our lives centers on our own needs. Forgive our impatience with those who are becoming more vulnerable with age. Teach us to create space in our schedule and in our home to reach out to the elderly whom you love. Help us to recognize those who need love, attention, or appreciation. Give us courage and compassion to reach out to someone who might feel lonely or afraid of being a burden. Transform us so that our family may be a place of joyful embrace between young and old.

Raising Our Children

Parents as Teachers and Evangelists

The First Teachers of the Faith

The Bible . . . presents the family as the place where children are brought up in the faith. . . . One of the Psalms celebrates the proclamation of faith within families: "All that we have heard and known, that our fathers have told us, we will not hide from their children, but tell to the coming generation the glorious deeds of the Lord, and his might, and the wonders which he has wrought . . . that the next generation might know them, the children yet unborn, and arise and tell them to their children" (*Ps* 78:3-6). The family is thus the place where parents become their children's first teachers in the faith. They learn this "trade," passing it down from one person to another.

— *AMORIS LAETITIA*, 16

—— • *Reflect* • ——

Do you recall learning to pray and coming to understand your faith with your parents? How can you teach your own children to have a relationship with Christ and his Church?

—— • *Pray* • ——

Father, lead us as we try to bring our family closer to you. Help us notice the "teachable moments" in our family life that are opportunities to lead our children toward you. Show us how to teach our children to speak to you in prayer and to hear your voice within their hearts. Help us develop patterns of family prayer and Scripture reading so that we can pass on the richness that you have given us.

Family Prayer: A Few Simple Words

Family prayer is a special way of expressing and strengthening this paschal faith. A few minutes can be found each day to come together before the living God, to tell him our worries, to ask for the needs of our family, to pray for someone experiencing difficulty, to ask for help in showing love, to give thanks for life and for its blessings, and to ask Our Lady to protect us beneath her maternal mantle. With a few simple words, this moment of prayer can do immense good for our families.

—*AMORIS LAETITIA*, 318

—— • *Reflect* • ——

How do you pray together? How might you grow in bringing your worries and needs to God as a family?

—— • *Pray* • ——

Lord, please bless our family. Bring healing to those who are sick and comfort to those who are struggling. Hear our special intentions now for _____. Thank you for all our blessings, especially for _____. May we show our love for each other in practical ways and express our appreciation for each other's efforts. Holy Mary, pray for us, protect our family, and help us to grow in love.

The Power of Example

It is essential that children actually see that, for their parents, prayer is something truly important. Hence moments of family prayer and acts of devotion can be more powerful for evangelization than any catechism class or sermon.

—*AMORIS LAETITIA*, 288

—— • *Reflect* • ——

What practices of family prayer or devotion have been fruitful in your life? How can you begin to pray as a family, or what changes would benefit your current routine?

—— • *Pray* • ——

Lord Jesus, teach us to pray. Teach us to lead our children to you and help them learn to converse with you. Help us to make family prayer meaningful and enjoyable for all. Give us discernment as we seek the appropriate times, places, and practices to add to our family's pattern of life. Most of all, Lord, help us to meet you when we pray or read Scripture or receive the sacraments as a family. In all of these, bring us closer to you and your Church.

Passing On the Faith— Even in the Busyness

Raising children calls for an orderly process of handing on the faith. This is made difficult by current lifestyles, work schedules, and the complexity of today's world, where many people keep up a frenetic pace just to survive. Even so, the home must continue to be the place where we learn to appreciate the meaning and beauty of the faith, to pray and to serve our neighbor.

—*AMORIS LAETITIA*, 287

———— • *Reflect* • ————

How do the pace of life and conflicting priorities interfere with passing on the faith to your children? What works well to create a loving, faith-filled atmosphere at home?

———— • *Pray* • ————

Lord, we invite you into our busy family. Show us how to slow down and make time to "be" a family. Give us discernment on how we use our time. Help us to be faithful to family prayer and to the celebration of the Eucharist so that we can be fed by you. Show us how our family can reach out to those around us and serve our neighbors. May our faith be the foundation of our life together.

Interceding for Our Children

Handing on the faith presumes that parents themselves genuinely trust God, seek him, and sense their need for him, for only in this way does "one generation laud your works to another, and declare your mighty acts" (*Ps* 145:4) and "fathers make known to children your faithfulness" (*Is* 38:19). This means that we need to ask God to act in their hearts, in places where we ourselves cannot reach. A mustard seed, small as it is, becomes a great tree (cf. *Mt* 13:31-32); this teaches us to see the disproportion between our actions and their effects. We know that we do not own the gift, but that its care is entrusted to us. Yet our creative commitment is itself an offering which enables us to cooperate with God's plan.

—*AMORIS LAETITIA*, 287

• Reflect •

How do you and your spouse pray for your children? How might you grow in seeking God's blessing for your family?

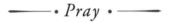

• Pray •

Lord, only you can touch the depths of our children's hearts. We ask you to come into their lives, enliven their faith, and draw our children closer to you. We try our best to teach them to know you and to live out your commands, but only you can make our efforts fruitful. We thank you for the children you have given to us as a trust. Teach us to love them and to nurture your life within them. Help us to pray regularly for our family.

Adolescents Need Witnesses of Faith

Education in the faith has to adapt to each child, since older resources and recipes do not always work. Children need symbols, actions, and stories. Since adolescents usually have issues with authority and rules, it is best to encourage their own experience of faith and to provide them with attractive testimonies that win them over by their sheer beauty. Parents desirous of nurturing the faith of their children are sensitive to their patterns of growth, for they know that spiritual experience is not imposed but freely proposed.

—*AMORIS LAETITIA*, 288

• *Reflect* •

How have the changing ages of your children required you to change your strategies for nurturing their faith? How can you provide "attractive testimonies" for your children?

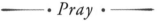

• *Pray* •

Father, you always find new ways to connect with your children. Help us to find creative ways to connect with ours. We want to teach them not only to know "about" you but to know you personally. Bring other faith-filled Catholics into their lives so that they can see in them an attractive witness of what it is to follow you. Make us joyful and true disciples so that we can help you form them into disciples as well.

Shielding Children from Harm

Parents need to consider what they want their children to be exposed to, and this necessarily means being concerned about who is providing their entertainment, who is entering their rooms through television and electronic devices, and with whom they are spending their free time. Only if we devote time to our children, speaking of important things with simplicity and concern, and finding healthy ways for them to spend their time, will we be able to shield them from harm. Vigilance is always necessary and neglect is never beneficial.

—*Amoris Laetitia*, 260

—— • *Reflect* • ——

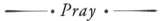

How have technology and media use affected your marriage and family? How can you capitalize on the benefits while curbing the negative effects of these powerful influences on your family?

—— • *Pray* • ——

Lord, give us wisdom as we discern our use of media. Help us to recognize times that media and virtual communication can displace the loving face-to-face interaction that you want to occur in our marriage and family. Give us courage to place wise boundaries around our own and our children's media use. Protect our home from pornography as well as the more subtle influences of the media that isolate us from each other and form our children's thinking in ways that will harm them. Help us to use media in positive ways to show our children what is important and beautiful in life.

Teaching Children to Ask for Forgiveness

It is also essential to help children and adolescents to realize that misbehavior has consequences. They need to be encouraged to put themselves in other people's shoes and to acknowledge the hurt they have caused. . . . It is important to train children firmly to ask forgiveness and to repair the harm done to others. As the educational process bears fruit in the growth of personal freedom, children come to appreciate that it was good to grow up in a family and even to put up with the demands that every process of formation makes.

—*AMORIS LAETITIA*, 268

——— • *Reflect* • ———

How do you go about teaching your children to ask for forgiveness in your family? How effective is it?

——— • *Pray* • ———

Father, we want to be a family that routinely asks for forgiveness of one another. Let us teach our children by what we do, letting them see us asking forgiveness of them or of our spouse when we have hurt them. Make us approachable so that our children have the courage to come to us and ask for pardon. Give us merciful hearts that embrace and quickly forgive our loved ones with open arms and hearts.

The Value of Learning How to Wait

In our own day, dominated by stress and rapid technological advances, one of the most important tasks of families is to provide an education in hope. This does not mean preventing children from playing with electronic devices, but rather finding ways to help them develop their critical abilities and not to think that digital speed can apply to everything in life. Postponing desires does not mean denying them but simply deferring their fulfillment. When children or adolescents are not helped to realize that some things have to be waited for, they can become obsessed with satisfying their immediate needs and develop the vice of "wanting it all now." This is a grand illusion which does not favor freedom but weakens it.

—*Amoris Laetitia*, 275

• *Reflect* •

How often do you delay gratifying your desires for the good of your family? How can you learn to wait for those things you want? Are you and your spouse actively teaching this virtue to your children?

• *Pray* •

Lord, give us the grace to be patient and willing to wait. May we defer the fulfillment of our immediate desires for the good of our family. Give us discernment and unity as we decide what to do with our time and money. Help us to model and teach patience to our children and to show them that good things are worth working for and waiting for.

Using Media to Connect,
Not Keep Apart

The educational process that occurs between parents and children can be helped or hindered by the increasing sophistication of the communications and entertainment media. When well used, these media can be helpful for connecting family members who live apart from one another. Frequent contacts help to overcome difficulties. Still, it is clear that these media cannot replace the need for more personal and direct dialogue, which requires physical presence or at least hearing the voice of the other person. We know that sometimes they can keep people apart rather than together, as when at dinnertime everyone is surfing on a mobile phone, or when one spouse falls asleep waiting for the other who spends hours playing with an electronic device.

—*AMORIS LAETITIA*, 278

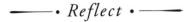

Reflect

How often does your family eat dinner together? How can you make dinnertime a time of fun and being present to one another?

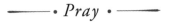

Pray

Lord Jesus, it was so important to you to be physically present to us that you became man, and now you are physically present to us daily in the Eucharist. Help us to be physically present to each other. Let our love grow as we enjoy meals and conversation. Remind us that these small steps are not a burden or a hassle but your gift to us to strengthen our love.

"Our Daily Love"

Reflections on 1 Corinthians 13

Love Means Being Slow to Anger

Love is patient. The first word used is *makrothyméi*. . . . Its meaning is clarified by the Greek translation of the Old Testament, where we read that God is "slow to anger" (*Ex* 34:6; *Num* 14:18). It refers, then, to the quality of one who does not act on impulse and avoids giving offense. We find this quality in the God of the Covenant, who calls us to imitate him also within the life of the family.

—*Amoris Laetitia*, 91

———— · *Reflect* · ————

How do you experience patient, merciful love in your family? How can you grow in showing it?

———— · *Pray* · ————

Merciful God, you are slow to anger and abounding in love. You welcome us even when we rebel against you and reject your love. Help us to be patient with each other and our family members, recognizing that they, too, are your beloved children. Help us to pray for those who irritate us. Do not allow bitterness or resentment to take root in our hearts toward anyone.

Compassion Means Accepting Others

Being patient does not mean letting ourselves be constantly mistreated, tolerating physical aggression, or allowing other people to use us. We encounter problems whenever we think that relationships or people ought to be perfect, or when we put ourselves at the center and expect things to turn out our way. Then everything makes us impatient, everything makes us react aggressively. Unless we cultivate patience, we will always find excuses for responding angrily. We will end up incapable of living together, antisocial, unable to control our impulses, and our families will become battlegrounds. That is why the word of God tells us: "Let all bitterness and wrath and anger and clamor and slander be put away from you, with all malice" (*Eph* 4:31). Patience takes root when I recognize that other people also have a right to live in this world, just as they are. It does not matter if they hold me back, if they unsettle my plans, or annoy me by the way they act or think, or if they are not everything I want them to be. Love always has an aspect of deep compassion that leads to accepting the other person as part of this world, even when he or she acts differently than I would like.

— *Amoris Laetitia*, 92

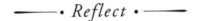 *Reflect*

How often do you put yourself at the center and expect things to turn out as you wish? What attitudes could you adopt that would help you be more patient and compassionate?

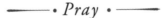 *Pray*

Holy Spirit, we don't want to react impatiently and aggressively. When we are tempted in this way, show us the truth: that other people have a right to live in this world just as they are. We repent of those times when we have treated others without mercy and compassion. Forgive us and give us the grace to be as patient as you are with us.

Humility toward the Unsure and Weak

It is important for Christians to show their love by the way they treat family members who are less knowledgeable about the faith, weak, or less sure in their convictions. At times the opposite occurs: the supposedly mature believers within the family become unbearably arrogant.

—*AMORIS LAETITIA*, 98

———— • *Reflect* • ————

How can you show greater patience and humility toward family members who may not have the same experience and knowledge of the faith that you have? How can you allow others to teach you more about God?

———— • *Pray* • ————

Humble Jesus, you emptied yourself and became a man. You learned everything from your Father in heaven and from your parents and teachers. Give us humble hearts. Remind us that we have much to learn. Help us be slow to speak and quick to listen to others. Remind us that the maturity of our faith is measured not by what we know but, rather, by the way we love. As we seek to grow in humility, we trust in your merciful love.

Speaking with Gentleness

To be open to a genuine encounter with others, "a kind look" is essential. This is incompatible with a negative attitude that readily points out other people's shortcomings while overlooking one's own. A kind look helps us to see beyond our own limitations, to be patient and to cooperate with others, despite our differences. . . . Those who love are capable of speaking words of comfort, strength, consolation, and encouragement. These were the words that Jesus himself spoke: "Take heart, my son!" (*Mt* 9:2); "Great is your faith!" (*Mt* 15:28); "Arise!" (*Mk* 5:41); "Go in peace" (*Lk* 7:50); "Be not afraid" (*Mt* 14:27). These are not words that demean, sadden, anger, or show scorn. In our families, we must learn to imitate Jesus' own gentleness in our way of speaking to one another.

—*AMORIS LAETITIA*, 100

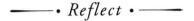

——— • *Reflect* • ———

How do you speak to your spouse and children? Are your attitudes and words gentle and loving? How often do they build up or tear down?

——— • *Pray* • ———

Jesus, help us to view our family through eyes of kindness. Curb our tongue so that we speak words of comfort and encouragement instead of harsh words that demean our loved ones. Transform our hearts to be like yours so that our words strengthen one another and our children rather than tear them down.

Love Means Not Being Irritable

Love is not irritable or resentful. [T]he word . . .
paroxýnetai has to do more with an interior indignation provoked by something from without. It refers
to a violent reaction within, a hidden irritation that
sets us on edge where others are concerned, as if
they were troublesome or threatening and thus to be
avoided. To nurture such interior hostility helps no
one. It only causes hurt and alienation. Indignation is
only healthy when it makes us react to a grave injus-
tice; when it permeates our attitude towards others
it is harmful.

—*AMORIS LAETITIA*, 103

—— • *Reflect* • ——

What irritates you? What are the things that you do that irritate your spouse? What is a helpful strategy for handling feelings of irritation so that they don't create a wedge between you?

—— • *Pray* • ——

Loving Father, you are never annoyed with us, nor do you ever give us the cold shoulder. Instead, you only want to draw closer to us and to bless us. Transform our hearts so that we recognize hostility when it rises up inside of us. Help us turn to you in situations when we feel irritated with one another. Fill us with your grace so that we can love others as you love us.

Do Not Nurture Anger

The Gospel tells us to look to the log in our own eye (cf. *Mt* 7:5). Christians cannot ignore the persistent admonition of God's word not to nurture anger: "Do not be overcome by evil" (*Rom* 12:21). "Let us not grow weary in doing good" (*Gal* 6:9). It is one thing to sense a sudden surge of hostility and another to give into it, letting it take root in our hearts: "Be angry but do not sin; do not let the sun go down on your anger" (*Eph* 4:26). My advice is never to let the day end without making peace in the family. "And how am I going to make peace? By getting down on my knees? No! Just by a small gesture, a little something, and harmony within your family will be restored. Just a little caress, no words are necessary. But do not let the day end without making peace in your family" (Catechesis, May 13, 2015).

—*AMORIS LAETITIA*, 104

—— · *Reflect* · ——

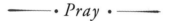

How often do you go to bed without making peace with your spouse? How can you restore peace with your words or actions of love? Do you need to repent for nurturing anger or hurting your spouse?

—— · *Pray* · ——

Merciful Father, you are always ready to forgive. Give us hearts that are slow to anger and quick to forgive. Thank you for the gift of one another. Help us to express our love for each other every day. May we refuse to allow bitterness or coldness to remain between us. Remind us to end each day with a word or gesture of love and mercy.

React to Annoyance with a Blessing

Our first reaction when we are annoyed should be one of heartfelt blessing, asking God to bless, free, and heal that person. "On the contrary, bless, for to this you have been called, that you may obtain a blessing" (*1 Pet 3:9*).

—*AMORIS LAETITIA*, 104

—— • *Reflect* • ——

What is your first reaction when you feel annoyed?
How can you learn to pause and respond with
prayer and blessing?

—— • *Pray* • ——

Lord, you are slow to anger and abounding in love.
Whenever we feel annoyed with someone, remind us
that everyone is fighting hidden battles that we know
nothing about. Help us to stop and pray a blessing
for that person instead of saying things we will later
regret. Make us vehicles of your peace. Lord, you
know exactly which people annoy each of us the
most. We ask you to bless those people today. Give
us a chance to show them your love.

Rooting Out Resentment

Once we allow ill will to take root in our hearts, it leads to deep resentment. . . . [L]ove "takes no account of evil"; "it is not resentful." The opposite of resentment is forgiveness, which is rooted in a positive attitude that seeks to understand other people's weaknesses and to excuse them. As Jesus said, "Father, forgive them; for they know not what they do" (*Lk* 23:34). Yet we keep looking for more and more faults, imagining greater evils, presuming all kinds of bad intentions, and so resentment grows and deepens. Thus, every mistake or lapse on the part of a spouse can harm the bond of love and the stability of the family.

—*AMORIS LAETITIA*, 105

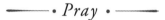

· Reflect ·

Do you keep a record of your spouse's wrongs? How does this affect how you relate to your husband or wife and interpret their behavior? How can you instead keep a record of your spouse's positive attributes at the forefront of your mind?

· Pray ·

Lord, your forgiveness and compassion are so great. Help us be understanding of the weaknesses of the other. Give us your grace so that we can choose to let go of all bitterness. Bring us to greater unity as we forgive each other. Fill us with your inexhaustible mercy and love.

Preserving Family Unity

When we have been offended or let down, forgiveness is possible and desirable, but no one can say that it is easy. The truth is that "family communion can only be preserved and perfected through a great spirit of sacrifice. It requires, in fact, a ready and generous openness of each and all to understanding, to forbearance, to pardon, to reconciliation. There is no family that does not know how selfishness, discord, tension, and conflict violently attack and at times mortally wound its own communion: hence there arise the many and varied forms of division in family life" (John Paul II, Apostolic Exhortation *Familiaris Consortio*, 21.).

—*AMORIS LAETITIA*, 106

———— • *Reflect* • ————

How have you experienced division in your family life? In what ways would forgiveness and sacrifice open the door to restoring unity?

———— • *Pray* • ————

Lord Jesus, as a man you experienced the disappointment and hurt that human relationships bring, yet you continually looked beyond the faults and saw the person. Give our family your spirit of generous forgiveness. Teach us to recognize the great dignity of our spouse and our children and their capacity for future goodness. Help us to give them the gift of forgiveness that you have given to each of us. Lord, make us one.

Forgiving Ourselves and Our Past Mistakes

Today we recognize that being able to forgive others implies the liberating experience of understanding and forgiving ourselves. Often our mistakes, or criticism we have received from loved ones, can lead to a loss of self-esteem. We become distant from others, avoiding affection and fearful in our interpersonal relationships. Blaming others becomes falsely reassuring. We need to learn to pray over our past history, to accept ourselves, to learn how to live with our limitations, and even to forgive ourselves, in order to have this same attitude towards others.

—*AMORIS LAETITIA*, 107

——— • *Reflect* • ———

How difficult do you find it to accept your limitations? To forgive yourself for past mistakes? How could praying over your past history help?

——— • *Pray* • ———

Father in heaven, you see everything. On the cross, your Son bore in his own body the sins of the entire world. Lord, we are sinners; have mercy on us. Help us to accept your forgiveness and be healed of any self-loathing. Help us to forgive ourselves and to relinquish any blame or unforgiveness we may harbor toward our loved ones. We pray this in the name of your Son, Jesus.

Accepting God's Unconditional Love

We have known a love that is prior to any of our own efforts, a love that constantly opens doors, promotes, and encourages. If we accept that God's love is unconditional, that the Father's love cannot be bought or sold, then we will become capable of showing boundless love and forgiving others even if they have wronged us. Otherwise, our family life will no longer be a place of understanding, support, and encouragement, but rather one of constant tension and mutual criticism.

—*AMORIS LAETITIA*, 108

—— • *Reflect* • ——

When recently have you experienced God's unconditional love? How can this transform the way that you relate to your family, especially when someone wrongs you?

—— • *Pray* • ——

Merciful Father, your love is unchanging and without limit. You do not treat us as our sins deserve but look upon each of us with mercy and forgiveness. Help us to forgive family members, and one another, for the wrongs that have been done to us. We choose to let go of the hurts and grudges we have held. Pour your love into ours hearts so that, by your grace, we can see and love others the way you see and love them.

Rejoicing in the Happiness of Others

Our Lord especially appreciates those who find joy in the happiness of others. If we fail to learn how to rejoice in the well-being of others, and focus primarily on our own needs, we condemn ourselves to a joyless existence, for, as Jesus said, "It is more blessed to give than to receive" (*Acts* 20:35). The family must always be a place where, when something good happens to one of its members, they know that others will be there to celebrate it with them.

—*Amoris Laetitia*, 110

—— • *Reflect* • ——

How does your family celebrate each other's joys and accomplishments?

—— • *Pray* • ——

Lord, sometimes we struggle to rejoice in the good in another person's life and instead feel jealous. We want to be content with what we have and happy for those who are rejoicing. Help our family to focus on others and their needs, not our own. May we always make it a point to recognize and celebrate the joys and accomplishments of each family member in our daily life together.

The Fruit of Forbearance

Paul says that love "bears all things" (*panta stégei*). This is about more than simply putting up with evil; it has to do with *the use of the tongue*. The verb can mean "holding one's peace" about what may be wrong with another person. It implies limiting judgment, checking the impulse to issue a firm and ruthless condemnation: "Judge not and you will not be judged" (*Lk* 6:37).

—*Amoris Laetitia*, 112

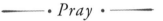

· Reflect ·

How do you speak to the other members of your family? How often is your speech characterized by restraint and love? By judgment and harshness?

· Pray ·

Holy Spirit, grow in me your fruit of forbearance. Let me be quick to listen and slow to speak. Help me to hold my tongue when I am tempted to make a harsh or judgmental comment. Help me to speak words that are encouraging and life-giving to my family. When I need to correct or disagree with someone, help me to speak respectfully and uphold the people I love.

Love Cherishes the Good Name of Others

Although it runs contrary to the way we normally use our tongues, God's word tells us: "Do not speak evil against one another, brothers and sisters" (*Jas* 4:11). Being willing to speak ill of another person is a way of asserting ourselves, venting resentment and envy without concern for the harm we may do. We often forget that slander can be quite sinful; it is a grave offense against God when it seriously harms another person's good name and causes damage that is hard to repair. Hence God's word forthrightly states that the tongue "is a world of iniquity" that "stains the whole body" (*Jas* 3:6); it is a "restless evil, full of deadly poison" (3:8). Whereas the tongue can be used to "curse those who are made in the likeness of God" (3:9), love cherishes the good name of others, even one's enemies. In seeking to uphold God's law we must never forget this specific requirement of love.

—*AMORIS LAETITIA*, 112

—— • *Reflect* • ——

How can you create a family culture in which another person is never spoken of negatively? Do you make a habit of guarding the good name even of those who oppose you or speak ill of you?

—— • *Pray* • ——

Holy Spirit, keep watch over our tongues so that we can be a family who blesses, not curses, others. Let this sweet spirit of love pervade every member of our family as we seek to assume the best of others and to find the good in them, not their faults. Father, may we remember how much you love all your children and desire that we do the same.

Speaking Well of Our Spouse

Married couples joined by love speak well of each other; they try to show their spouse's good side, not their weakness and faults. In any event, they keep silent rather than speak ill of them. This is not merely a way of acting in front of others; it springs from an interior attitude. Far from ingenuously claiming not to see the problems and weaknesses of others, it sees those weaknesses and faults in a wider context. It recognizes that these failings are a part of a bigger picture. We have to realize that all of us are a complex mixture of light and shadows. The other person is much more than the sum of the little things that annoy me. Love does not have to be perfect for us to value it. The other person loves me as best they can, with all their limits, but the fact that love is imperfect does not mean that it is untrue or unreal. It is real, albeit limited and earthly. If I expect too much, the other person will let me know, for he or she can neither play God nor serve all my needs. Love coexists

with imperfection. It "bears all things" and can hold
its peace before the limitations of the loved one.

—*AMORIS LAETITIA*, 113

 • *Reflect* •

Do you make it a habit of speaking well of your
spouse? How can you live at peace with your spouse's
limitations and your own?

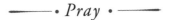 • *Pray* •

Lord, you "bear all things" and never stop loving us.
We don't have to be perfect in order for you to love
us. Help us to love each other, even when we do it
imperfectly. We want to see and love the goodness
in one another and appreciate the attempts that the
other makes to love us. Thank you for your unfail-
ing love, which makes up for our deficiencies and
meets all our needs.

Trusting in the Goodness of Others

Love believes all things. Here "belief" is not to be taken in its strict theological meaning, but more in the sense of what we mean by "trust." This goes beyond simply presuming that the other is not lying or cheating. Such basic trust recognizes God's light shining beyond the darkness, like an ember glowing beneath the ash.

—*AMORIS LAETITIA*, 114

—— • *Reflect* • ——

In what ways do you recognize God's light shining through your spouse and your children? How do you let God's light shine through you?

—— • *Pray* • ——

Lord, you have given us to one another as a special sign of your love and care. Sometimes it is easier to focus on each other's faults than to recognize the ways in which we bring your light to one another. Help us to believe in each other and in our children—to see the goodness you have placed there, and to trust that what you have begun in us, you will bring to completion.

Love Trusts and Sets Free

[T]rust enables a relationship to be free. It means we do not have to control the other person, to follow their every step lest they escape our grip. Love trusts, it sets free, it does not try to control, possess, and dominate everything. This freedom, which fosters independence, an openness to the world around us and to new experiences, can only enrich and expand relationships. The spouses then share with one another the joy of all they have received and learned outside the family circle. At the same time, this freedom makes for sincerity and transparency, for those who know that they are trusted and appreciated can be open and hide nothing. Those who know that their spouse is always suspicious, judgmental, and lacking unconditional love, will tend to keep secrets, conceal their failings and weaknesses, and pretend to be someone other than who they are. On the other hand, a family marked by loving trust, come what may, helps its members to be themselves and spontaneously to reject deceit, falsehood, and lies.

—*AMORIS LAETITIA*, 115

—— • *Reflect* • ——

How open and transparent are you with your spouse?
How does this help trust to grow?

—— • *Pray* • ——

Lord, we want to grow in trust of one another. Free
us from any fear that causes us to try to control one
another or to be suspicious of one another. Teach us
to be vulnerable, to show each other our truest self,
even our weaknesses or failures. Help us to respond
to each other's openness with unconditional love
and acceptance, trusting that we, too, are loved for
who we are.

God Makes Crooked Lines Straight

Love does not despair of the future. . . . [T]his phrase speaks of the hope of one who knows that others can change, mature, and radiate unexpected beauty and untold potential. This does not mean that everything will change in this life. It does involve realizing that, though things may not always turn out as we wish, God may well make crooked lines straight and draw some good from the evil we endure in this world.

—*AMORIS LAETITIA*, 116

—— • *Reflect* • ——

Where in your marriage do you need greater hope for the future? How can your relationship with God increase your hope for your life together?

—— • *Pray* • ——

Lord, you always have hope for us and in us. You see our potential even when we do not. Fill us with the hope and confidence that you can change each of us and bring goodness even out of suffering. Remind us that you are always present, even in our dark times, trying to draw us together as a couple and closer to you.

Seeing Others in the Light of Hope

Here hope comes most fully into its own, for it embraces the certainty of life after death. Each person, with all his or her failings, is called to the fullness of life in heaven. There, fully transformed by Christ's resurrection, every weakness, darkness, and infirmity will pass away. There the person's true being will shine forth in all its goodness and beauty. This realization helps us, amid the aggravations of this present life, to see each person from a supernatural perspective, in the light of hope, and await the fullness that he or she will receive in the heavenly kingdom, even if it is not yet visible.

—*Amoris Laetitia*, 117

——— · *Reflect* · ———

How often do I set my hope on the fullness of life awaiting us in heaven? How can I make an eternal perspective part of my daily life?

——— · *Pray* · ———

Lord, you are our hope. Thank you for your promise of eternal life with you, where all our brokenness will be fully transformed. Help our family to see each other from your heavenly perspective, as we will one day be, the way you created us to be. Allow that perspective to change our hearts so that we don't demand instant change, but rather patiently wait in the hope for you to finish your work in us.

Love Never Gives Up

Love endures all things. . . . This means that love bears every trial with a positive attitude. It stands firm in hostile surroundings. This "endurance" involves not only the ability to tolerate certain aggravations, but something greater: a constant readiness to confront any challenge. It is a love that *never gives up*, even in the darkest hour. It shows a certain dogged heroism, a power to resist every negative current, an irrepressible commitment to goodness.

—*AMORIS LAETITIA*, 118

The Christian ideal, especially in families, is a love that never gives up. I am sometimes amazed to see men or women who have had to separate from their spouse for their own protection, yet, because of their enduring conjugal love, still try to help them, even by enlisting others, in their moments of illness, suffering, or trial. Here too we see a love that never gives up.

—*AMORIS LAETITIA*, 119

· *Reflect* ·

Think of a current or past challenge that you have had to face. When were you tempted to give up? What helped you to stay the course?

· *Pray* ·

Lord Jesus, you endured even the cross because you kept your sights on the goodness of the Father and the glory of saving your people. Your love never fails or gives up on us. Help us to persevere in trials, no matter the cost. We want to be positive and fixed on your goodness, and the goodness of our marriage and family life, even in the face of challenges. Keep us faithful, Lord!

the WORD
among us®
The *Spirit* of Catholic Living

This book was published by The Word Among Us. Since 1981, The Word Among Us has been answering the call of the Second Vatican Council to help Catholic laypeople encounter Christ in the Scriptures.

The name of our company comes from the prologue to the Gospel of John and reflects the vision and purpose of all of our publications: to be an instrument of the Spirit, whose desire is to manifest Jesus' presence in and to the children of God. In this way, we hope to contribute to the Church's ongoing mission of proclaiming the gospel to the world so that all people would know the love and mercy of our Lord and grow more deeply in their faith as missionary disciples.

Our monthly devotional magazine, *The Word Among Us*, features meditations on the daily and Sunday Mass readings, and currently reaches more than one million Catholics in North America and another half million Catholics in one hundred countries around the world. Our book division, The Word Among Us Press, publishes numerous books, Bible studies, and pamphlets that help Catholics grow in their faith.

To learn more about who we are and what we publish, log on to our website at www.wau.org. There you will find a variety of Catholic resources that will help you grow in your faith.

Embrace His Word, Listen to God . . .

www.wau.org